Seven Inspirational Favorites for Two Pianos
ARRANGED BY MARILYN THOMPSON

MW01284861

Contents

Dedication

For Nielson and Young
in commemoration of 25 years of superb artistry as America's Beloved Duo Pianists
with warm memories of "Nielson and Young's Musical Europe"

Lillenas PUBLISHING COMPANY

KANSAS CITY, MO 64141

Just a Closer Walk with Thee

Anonymous
Arr. by Marilyn Thompson

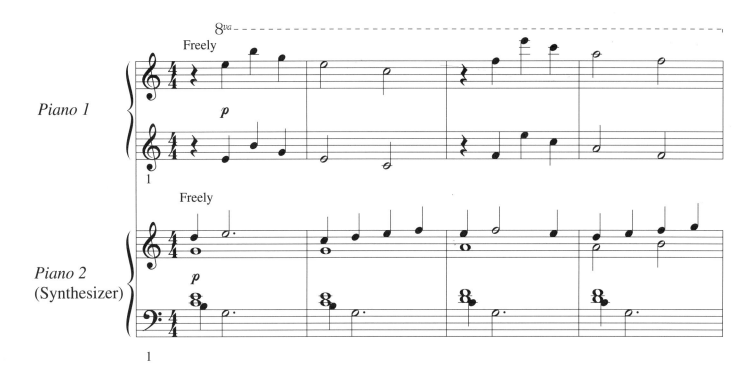

Let There Be Peace on Earth

SY MILLER & JILL JACKSON
Arr. by Marilyn Thompson

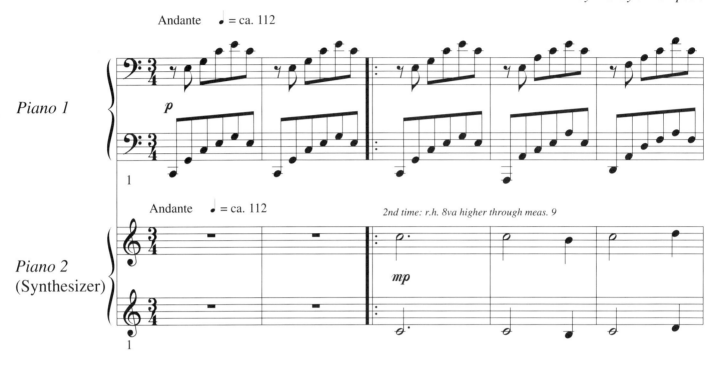

16

Give Me Jesus

Spiritual
Arr. by Marilyn Thompson

Piano 1

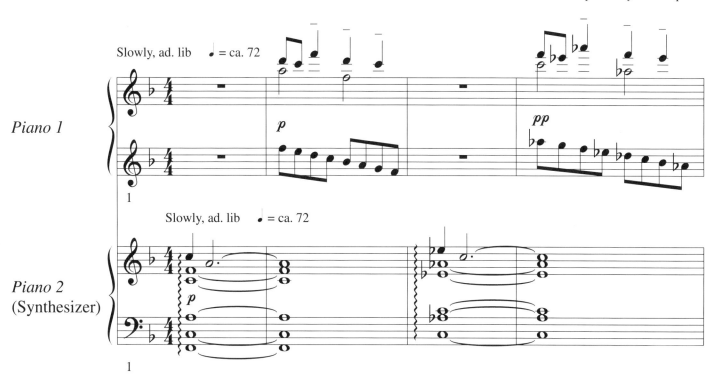

Piano 2
(Synthesizer)

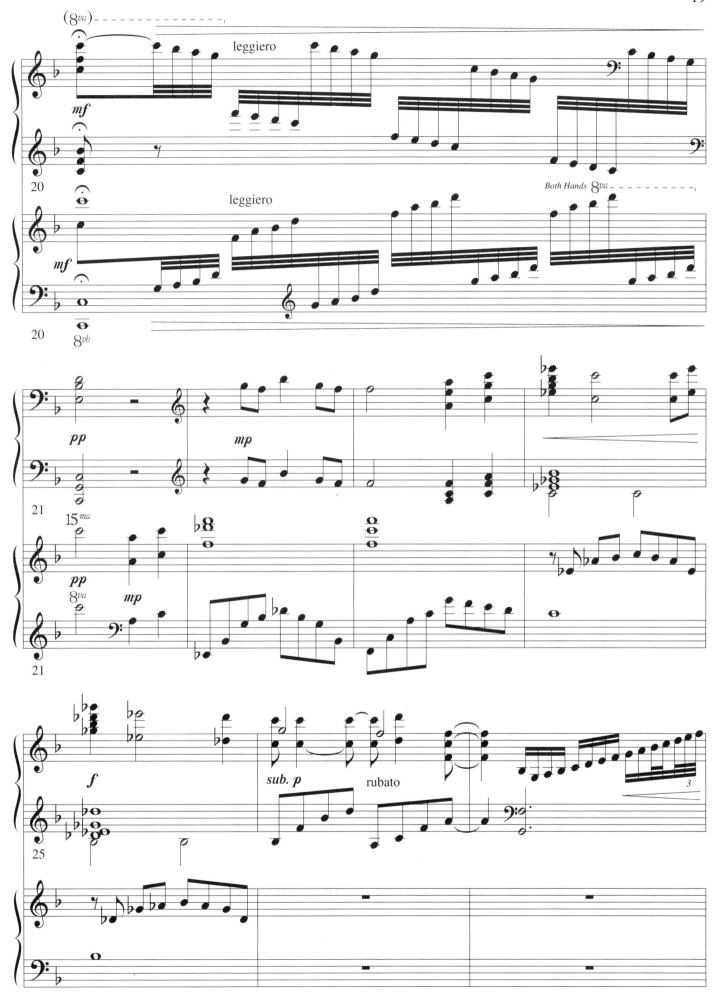

Poor Wayfaring Stranger

Spiritual
Arr. by Marilyn Thompson

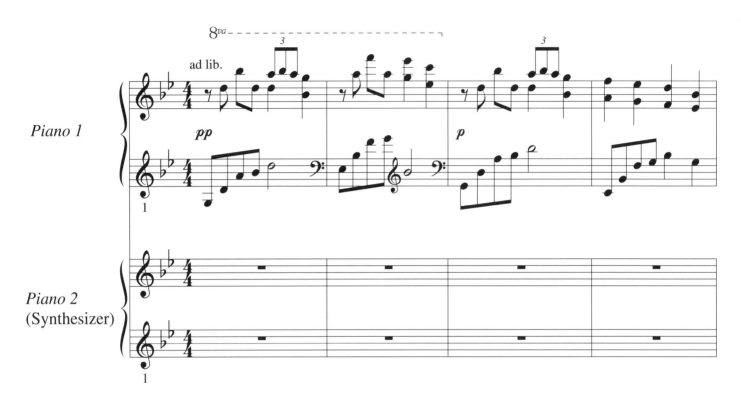

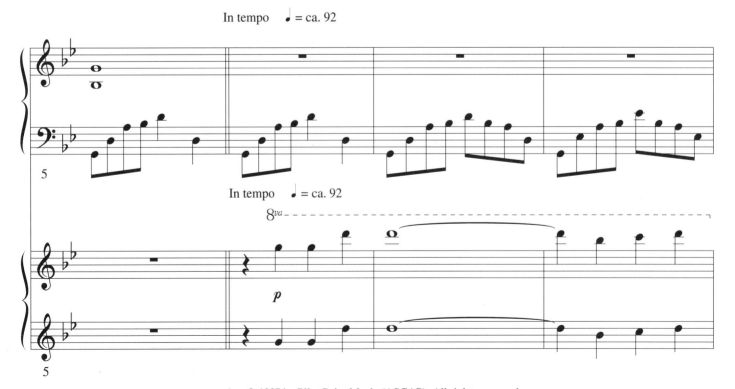

The Morning Trumpet

Early American Tune
Arr. by Marilyn Thompson

Overshadowed

GEORGE S. SCHULER
Arr. by Marilyn Thompson

Praise, My Soul, the King of Heaven

MARK ANDREWS
Arr. by Marilyn Thompson

Piano 1

Piano 2
(Synthesizer)